Sell Globally, Tax Locally

AEI STUDIES ON TAX REFORM
Kevin A. Hassett
Series Editor

ASSESSING THE EFFECTIVENESS OF SAVING INCENTIVES
R. Glenn Hubbard and Jonathan S. Skinner

CUTTING TAXES FOR INSURING: OPTIONS AND EFFECTS
OF TAX CREDITS FOR HEALTH INSURANCE
Mark V. Pauly and Bradley Herring

DISTRIBUTIONAL IMPLICATIONS OF A CONSUMPTION TAX
William M. Gentry and R. Glenn Hubbard

THE EFFECTS OF RECENT TAX REFORM ON LABOR SUPPLY
Thomas J. Kniesner and James P. Ziliak

FUNDAMENTAL ISSUES IN CONSUMPTION TAXATION
David F. Bradford

FUNDAMENTAL TAX REFORM AND CORPORATE FINANCE
William M. Gentry and R. Glenn Hubbard

SELL GLOBALLY, TAX LOCALLY:
SALES TAX REFORM FOR THE NEW ECONOMY
Michael S. Greve

TAX POLICY AND INVESTMENT
Kevin A. Hassett

TAXATION OF FINANCIAL SERVICES
UNDER A CONSUMPTION TAX
Peter R. Merrill

TAXING CONSUMPTION IN A GLOBAL ECONOMY
Harry Grubert and T. Scott Newlon

TAXING INTERNATIONAL BUSINESS INCOME:
DIVIDEND EXEMPTION VERSUS THE CURRENT SYSTEM
Harry Grubert and John Mutti

Sell Globally, Tax Locally

Sales Tax Reform for the New Economy

Michael S. Greve

The AEI Press

Publisher for the American Enterprise Institute

WASHINGTON, D.C.

2003

336, 2713
683 a

Available in the United States from the AEI Press, c/o Client Distribution Services, 193 Edwards Drive, Jackson, TN 38301. To order, call toll free: 1-800-343-4499. Distributed outside the United States by arrangement with Eurospan, 3 Henrietta Street, London WC2E 8LU, England.

1 3 5 7 9 10 8 6 4 2

Printed in the United States of America

Contents

Foreword

Economists have reached a broad consensus concerning the appearance of an optimal tax system. Such a system would have a very broad base—perhaps limited to consumption—and marginal tax rates as low as revenue demands will allow. While there is general agreement concerning those basic features of an optimal tax system, significant disagreement remains concerning the size of the benefits to be gained from a fundamental reform that would replace the current system of high marginal tax rates with one that conformed closely to the prescriptions of theory. Disagreement also abounds concerning the distributional impact of fundamental tax reforms. The lack of professional consensus undoubtedly discourages would-be reformers, who for more than a decade have shied away from fundamental fixes and instead tinkered endlessly with a system that has increased steadily in complexity.

With this state of affairs in mind, we at AEI have organized a tax reform seminar series since January 1996. At each seminar, an economist presents original research designed to bring consensus concerning the costs and benefits of fundamental tax reform one step closer. Recent topics include transition problems in moving to a consumption tax, the effects of consumption taxation on housing and the stock market, the distributional impact of tax reforms, the effect of privatizing Social Security on the long-term budget outlook, and the international tax implications of fundamental reform.

The goal of this pamphlet series is to distribute the best research on economic issues in tax reform to as broad an audience as possible. Each publication reflects not only the insights of the authors, but also the helpful comments and criticisms of seminar participants—economists, attorneys, accountants, and journalists in the tax policy community.

KEVIN A. HASSETT
American Enterprise Institute

1

Introduction

The tax treatment of cross-border sales, both in the United States and abroad, is uniformly decried as terribly complex, burdensome, and inefficient. Administrative and enforcement problems are particularly acute in the rapidly growing area of electronic commerce. Those problems are compounded by inequities and economic distortions. As currently constructed, the system effectively allows many Internet sales and other remote transactions (such as catalogue sales) to escape taxation, depriving governments of revenues and giving Internet sellers an unwarranted advantage over competing, more traditional industries.

Reform proposals, advanced principally by governments and intergovernmental institutions and supported by industries that feel threatened by the growing e-commerce sector, run toward intergovernmental tax harmonization and simplification. The political economy in the e-tax arena will likely produce *some* tax harmonization. For reasons discussed in this paper, however, those mechanisms will not be nearly as efficient or equitable as their supporters hope (nor, candidly, quite as oppressive as their opponents fear). For reasons explained in this paper, they will likely make sales taxation even more burdensome, complex, and expensive, to little or no offsetting benefit. That expectation, coupled with the fact that the existing tax regime is uniformly considered an absurd imposition on national and international commerce, creates both reasons and room to consider alternatives

The author wishes to thank Kate Crawford for helpful comments and research assistance, and Jonathan Klick, Kevin Hassett, Peter R. Merrill, and Daniel Shaviro for exceptionally helpful comments.

to the status quo and its "harmonization." This paper presents one such reform proposal: origin-based sales taxation. Such a system, it is argued, may well increase beneficial competition between jurisdictions.

From Destination to Origin

Cross-border sales—through the Internet or any other channel—can be taxed either on the basis of their *destination* (the buyer's domicile) or their *origin* (the seller's home state or country). The e-commerce debate has unfolded against the background of an international and national consumption tax system that is largely based on the destination principle. That system is unworkable.

Under any destination-based regime, governments typically find it impossible to collect consumption taxes from purchasers. Hence, they must use the sellers of goods and services as a chokepoint and collection agent. That imperative entails two consequences:

- Because destination-based taxation compels sellers to calculate, report, and remit consumption taxes for each jurisdiction in which sales occur, it generates extravagant compliance costs, especially for smaller and medium-sized firms.[1] Even with the best intentions (and the best tax software), companies find it inordinately difficult to determine their tax remittance obligations in thousands of jurisdictions with different and constantly changing tax rates, definitions, and reporting requirements. Tax authorities, for their part, confront a regime of daunting administrative complexity. An origin-based system in principle can reduce these costs.

- Destination-based taxation requires a high degree of intergovernmental cooperation, since the imposition and enforcement of tax collection obligations on sellers who conduct their business abroad often require their home government's cooperation. The only equilibria under a destination-based regime, moreover, are perfect collusion among *all* governments or competition that drives each government to the same set of policies. A government that withholds its consent effectively places its domestic firms beyond the reach of foreign tax collectors and, in that manner, hands them a competitive advantage vis-à-vis others that have joined a cooperative. Both in the United States and internationally, this free rider problem has bedeviled attempts to generate government consensus on destination-based taxation.

It is universally acknowledged that destination-based taxation poses particularly serious practical problems in an e-commerce context. One sign of how serious these problems are is the absence of any resolution of the problem after many years of increasing Internet traffic.   Government authorities and traditional retail industries argue, however, that a selective departure from the destination principle in that context would create unjustifiable distortions between e-commerce and sales through conventional channels. (Conventional retailers would have to collect sales taxes. Internet sellers would not, thus handing them a pricing advantage.) Thus, those constituencies argue, we should make destination-based taxation "work" for e-commerce, principally through tax simplification and technological innovation (so as to reduce compliance and administrative costs) and, foremost, through enhanced intergovernmental cooperation and harmonization.

While this problem may have been foisted upon tax economists by the Internet, the general framework is one that legal scholars concerned with federalism have studied in different contexts for many years. Drawing on that work, this paper argues that the quest for a workable destination-based sales tax system is futile at best, and possibly destructive. Most importantly, the proposed solution relies upon the existence of a benevolent and rational super-governmental body for which there is no precedent. Its proponents profess allegiance to widely accepted principles of taxation—simplicity, neutrality among industries, and ease of administration. Destination-based taxation, however, cannot satisfy those principles, and in fact brings them into conflict. Although that tendency does not arise from the peculiar characteristics of e-commerce, it is particularly acute in that context. As shown below, extant harmonization proposals may well exacerbate the difficulties.

Instead of further extending the already unworkable destination approach to e-commerce, I explore the alternative of moving to an origin-based taxation for *all* sales, through all channels, here and abroad. Under an origin-based regime, each sale would be taxed once, at the same rate, by a single authority—the seller's home state or country. Origin-based taxation may well be preferable on the grounds of the very principles to which proponents of destination-based taxation profess allegiance: It is neutral among industries and more easily administered in part because it minimizes the need for government coordination and cooperation. Thus, a workable origin-based system would not depend upon unprecedented political accomplishments.

The Salience of Institutional Considerations

The nature and scope of this argument deserve clarification. First, the proposal is not intended as a contribution to, or step toward, a more comprehensive tax reform scheme. For example, advocates of a national sales tax—as a substitute for the existing tax code—may conclude that this paper misses the true point (or perhaps provides yet more fodder for radical reform canons). Arguments about the basic tax structure, however, are beyond the scope of this paper. For better or worse, the national and international debate over sales taxation has moved within more limited parameters. This paper accepts those confines and argues within them.

Second, I do not argue that origin-based sales taxation is more "efficient" than destination-based taxation, in the technical senses in which tax economists use that term. To anticipate a point discussed below, I recognize that origin-based sales taxes are viewed with great suspicion by tax economists who place a high premium on "locational neutrality"—that is, the notion that the tax system should not unduly distort private economic decisions.[2] I am inclined to think that this argument owes its force chiefly to its high level of theoretical abstraction. The central point of this paper, however, is not to argue with tax economists and their models but rather to persuade readers of the salience of institutional considerations that have been underestimated in the debate. Those arguments can be summarized as follows:

- Suppose that origin-based sales taxation can be shown to be inefficient in a strict economic sense: No economist would defend the *existing* destination-based system as efficient in that same strict sense. For institutional reasons, it is unlikely that extant harmonization proposals will create or even approximate a (technically) efficient destination-based system. If that is right, a sensible choice is to pick a system that promises to reduce enforcement and compliance costs. Origin-based taxation, relative to its rival, holds that promise.

- As a general rule, tax competition is preferable to an intergovernmental tax cartel. Origin-based taxation enhances the former, whereas destination-based taxation produces the latter.

- Origin-based taxation limits the coercive reach of each jurisdiction to its own citizens and businesses. Destination-based taxation, in contrast, systematically reaches across borders and, moreover, requires intergovernmental agreement to facilitate such mutual transgressions. We should be loath to pay that price—the direct and unavoidable cost of destination-based taxation—even if destination-based taxes could otherwise be shown to be efficient in some technical sense.

- Even if the origin principle were somehow wrong in the context of transaction taxes, it is unquestionably right for many issues of multi-jurisdictional Internet *regulation*.[3]

Setting a good precedent for those debates—where the destination principle would let the most restrictive or spiteful jurisdiction dictate the terms of regulation for the entire world—is another pragmatic reason for championing origin-based taxation.

Jointly and severally, these considerations do not clinch the case for origin-based sales taxation. They do, however, create a powerful presumption in its favor.

Presumptions, to be sure, usually come straight from the lawyer's trick bag. In fact, though, the sales tax debate already abounds with the poison. Origin-based sales taxation has been proposed in the tax literature,[4] by think tanks,[5] and in some political venues.[6] The response to those advances has been distinctly hostile. The reasons, however, have little to do with tax theory. They all converge on a single point—a fear that origin-based taxation might reduce state and local (and, in an international context, national) revenues. But the notion that origin-based taxation should be off the table *for no other reason than that it is not revenue-neutral or -enhancing* also is a presumption. In the end, the force of a presumption depends on the force of the arguments behind it. That test, not the suggestion of a presumption per se, should be the test of the case presented in this paper.

Brief Outline

The first part of this paper describes the status of the debate over the taxation of cross-border sales and explains why harmonization efforts in both international and domestic arenas are unlikely to produce a sensible regime. The second part of the paper makes a tentative case for origin-based sales taxation, with particular emphasis on the institutional considerations just outlined. The paper concludes with a discussion of the political context and suggests that a limited experiment with origin-based sales taxation is both viable and advisable.

2

The Elusive Quest for Harmonization

The domestic e-tax debate will by now strike many readers as familiar to the point of ennui. The inherent difficulties and dilemmas of destination-based taxation may thus appear in sharper relief in the less-familiar international context. The e-tax debate in the Organisation for Economic Co-operation and Development (OECD), the European Union (EU), and other international bodies differs in some respects from the domestic debate. Its structure and political economy, however, are substantially identical.

International organizations have devoted considerable attention to the problems of taxing electronic commerce. As in the American debate, government institutions have emphasized the need for tax harmonization and international cooperation in enforcement. The EU has been the leading advocate of that position, although individual member-countries have differed in their degree of enthusiasm. As in the United States, a few governments have resisted that clarion call. In international negotiations, the United States has often—though not consistently—opposed the push for harmonization and cooperation.

In contrast to the U.S. debate, which concerns the taxation of tangible goods, the international debate has concentrated almost entirely on the taxation of intangible goods and services. Such exchanges constitute only a tiny fraction of international e-commerce, let alone all commerce. A single reason explains the international preoccupation with this unlikely sector: Governments have found it exceedingly difficult to identify a reliable tax collector for electronic services.

The OECD and the Problem of the Remote Haircut

The OECD has discussed Internet commerce under the so-called Ottawa principles, agreed upon in 1998. The OECD's averred principles are tax neutrality between e-commerce and conventional commerce, administrative efficiency, certainty and simplicity, effectiveness and fairness, and flexibility in adjusting tax regimes to novel technologies and market conditions.[7] Crucially, the OECD also insists that consumption taxes should be levied at the place of consumption, as distinct from the place of origin of the good or service.[8] In other words, the OECD officially insists on destination-based taxation.

The application of these principles to electronic commerce poses great difficulties. The most vexing problems arise from the already-mentioned fact that while governments can tax consumption, they are rarely able to collect the tax from consumers. Thus, collection obligations must be imposed on the seller of a particular product or service. Such collection is possible—typically without extensive intergovernmental cooperation—so long as the taxing jurisdiction has a controllable chokepoint. Tangible goods provide that convenience: they can be intercepted and taxed at the border, regardless of whether the good was purchased through the Internet or some other channel. Intangible goods or services, in contrast, escape physical border controls.

A consulting or other such service provided through the Internet (or other means of remote communication) differs from a taxable haircut, for example, in two ways. First, the place of consumption is not necessarily the place where the customer receives the service or derives value from it. The seller, for his part, may have no easy way of verifying the customer's physical location. The OECD has acknowledged that a pure place of consumption test would impose "a significant, and in some instances an impossible, compliance burden" on remote service providers.[9] For the time being, the OECD has recommended a rough proxy: the place of consumption should be the country of the recipient's business presence or, for individual consumers, their "usual jurisdiction of residence." Even that determination, of course, becomes problematic when the buyer resides principally in cyberspace. Thus, the OECD has acknowledged that "further work is required on appropriate means of verifying" the customer's residence.[10]

Second, the hairdresser typically lives—or at any rate delivers the service—in the taxing jurisdiction. This enables the government to turn him into a collection agent. In cross-border transactions, in contrast, the service provider resides and operates in a different country. The attendant difficulties are typically manageable with respect to so-called B2B services—that is, services sold by one business to another. Under the Value Added Tax (VAT) systems administered by European countries, a firm's receipt of taxable services is a business expense that reduces reportable income. Since firms have an incentive to report B2B services, self-assessment and "reverse charges" will ensure relatively reliable tax reporting and collection.[11] The ultimate consumers, of course, have no such incentive. Thus, with respect to B2C commerce (that is, services sold to consumers), taxation at the place of consumption means that collection, reporting, and remittance obligations will fall on parties in foreign jurisdictions. Hence, the question that has driven the entire international e-tax debate: How can tax authorities reach the foreign sellers of Internet consumer services?

Foreign sellers—almost by definition—have *some* linkage to the jurisdiction where their services are consumed, which might in some instances permit an imposition of tax collection obligations. Along those lines, the EU at one point considered the option of refusing to enforce intellectual property rights for e-commerce products sold inside the EU by non-complying, non-EU firms. Such strategies, however, pose serious legal obstacles and diplomatic dangers. (The EU abandoned this plan, recognizing that the taxable firm might not actually own the intellectual property rights.)[12]

The only plausible (and permissible) chokepoint is the foreign seller's physical presence—through an office or a subsidiary—in the taxing jurisdiction. Foreign firms presumably attach some economic value to that presence, and they may tolerate an expropriation of that value and submit to tax collection obligations—up to a point. That point, though, is hard to identify. In any event, for sellers without any in-country presence, the imposition of collection and remittance obligations requires the cooperation of the service provider's jurisdiction.

The OECD has committed itself to a post-Ottawa agenda of "developing options for ensuring the continued effective administration and collection of consumption taxes."[13] While that endeavor is to be undertaken in a spirit of cooperation and consultation among governments and affected industries, the actual agenda is the construction of intergovernmental mechanisms for the collection of consumption taxes on international B2C services. The OECD has entrusted that process to its Committee on Financial Affairs (CFA).

Post-Ottawa, the CFA and its subcommittees have examined several options. In particular, in an effort to reduce industry resistance to destination-based taxation, the OECD committees studied technological options to decrease the compliance costs that sellers would confront under a destination-based system— but found that such technologies are currently unavailable.[14] For the time being, the OECD favors "some form of registration-based mechanism for B2C transactions," meaning that foreign sellers should voluntarily register for tax reporting and payment obligations in the country where their services were purchased. The OECD acknowledges that this system "has its shortcomings"—for the affected industries, inordinate compliance costs; for governments, substantial underreporting and enforcement problems.[15]

Even so, the OECD remains confident of its general direction. Some business sectors have argued for a zero tax rate, observing that B2C commerce—and especially B2C commerce carried on from wholly remote locations—constitutes only a tiny fraction of international commerce and of OECD countries' revenues. OECD bodies have rejected those proposals with uncharacteristic clarity. The no-tax option, the OECD has proclaimed, would generate an intolerable preference for e-commerce, while the alternative of zero taxation for all transborder services (through whatever channel) would produce an "unacceptable erosion of the tax base."[16] The OECD's insistence on tax neutrality between electronic and conventional commerce, coupled with its insistence on protecting each country's local tax base, dictates the organization's agenda—a single-minded search for viable B2C tax collection mechanisms. Those, in turn, will "necessitate a very strong level of administrative cooperation" among member-countries' tax authorities.[17] The OECD is committed to generating that cooperation.

Destination Taxes for Thee: The European Union

The EU's thinking about e-commerce taxation has developed in tandem with the OECD's. More precisely, the OECD has served as a quasi-global stage for the EU and its member-states' e-commerce ambitions. The EU formulated its e-commerce position in anticipation of the Ottawa Conference, where the OECD adopted the EU's principles without major change or qualification. But while the OECD and its various committees have since kept talking, the EU has put its policies into practice—unilaterally, as it were, and in a rather dramatic form.

In May 2002, the EU's Council of Ministers adopted amendments to the so-called Sixth VAT Directive.[18] The new rules, which took effect on July 1, 2003, address "electronically supplied services" (not goods) provided by non-EU firms to parties inside the EU. The amendments subject such services to the VAT. At the same time, the new rules exempt from the VAT services that are supplied by EU businesses to parties outside the EU.

The directive reiterates the EU's long-standing position that items of value provided through the Internet should be considered services, rather than goods. It adopts a broad understanding of "services," including (among other things) website supply and maintenance; software and upgrades; the supply of images, text, and information; provision of database access; and distance teaching—anything transmitted through the Internet for consideration. (The directive helpfully clarifies that the exchange of e-mails *per se* does not constitute an "electronically supplied service.") Unlike proposals floated earlier by the EU, the directive contains no *de minimis* exemption for small firms or low-volume sales. Every service and firm is subject to the tax scheme. This may include, for example, individual e-Bay sellers.

For business-to-business commerce, the VAT on electronic services is administered through self-assessment by the European business receiving the service (whether from inside or outside the EU). The rules for B2C services—that is, services provided to individual customers inside the EU—are considerably more complicated:

- If the seller has a permanent establishment in an EU country and supplies consumers from outside the EU, it must register and account for the VAT in each EU country where it supplies services. If such a firm supplies services from its European establishment, it will owe VAT in the country where its establishment is located.

- Firms without a fixed European establishment may choose to register with a single country inside the EU for VAT reporting and payment purposes. The country of registration will distribute the proceeds to each member country. Registered firms must file VAT returns each quarter. They must report their total sales and VAT due for each EU country where sales have been made, and they must retain their records for ten years. Evasion of tax and reporting obligation may entail deregistration of the business as well as civil and criminal prosecution by the country of registration or the country where the VAT has been or should have been paid.

The EU shouts its commitment to tax neutrality—among e-commerce and conventional sales, and among sellers from different countries—from the rooftops. The e-commerce amendments to the VAT Directive, however, conspicuously fail to accomplish that objective. The point bears emphasis: *Internally, with respect to services supplied from EU countries to EU consumers, the EU generally administers an origin-based tax regime.* Each firm must report and pay the VAT only once—in its home country. The applicable rate is that of the origin country (except for services rendered to non-EU customers, where the applicable rate is zero). Non-EU firms with a physical presence inside the EU will enjoy the same treatment. Not so, however, with entirely foreign firms: they will be subject to the rules of the *destination* country. Thus, a Luxembourg firm, or a U.S. firm with an office in that country, will pay a 15 percent VAT for services rendered anywhere in the EU, including Sweden. A U.S. firm without a European presence—even one that chooses Luxembourg as its country of registration—will, for the same service to the same Swedish customer, owe Sweden's VAT of 25 percent.

Leading e-commerce firms outside the EU—U.S. firms, specifically—have complained vociferously about the EU's directive. They have found an open ear at the U.S. Treasury Department, which protested the EU policy prior to its enactment and is now warily monitoring the implementation.[19] The department has complained both about the inordinate compliance costs that the EU has chosen to inflict and about the infringement on tax neutrality between EU and non-EU firms.[20] As a matter of economics, the American complaints seem overwrought: The volume of B2C e-commerce is small; the disadvantages suffered by U.S. firms vis-à-vis low-VAT firms in the European market may be compensated by competitive advantages vis-à-vis Swedish firms; U.S. firms sell electronic services that cannot be obtained from European firms at any price; and the establishment of a parity-ensuring European presence (for American firms that do significant business in Europe) is a relatively low-cost proposition. The point of the American objections is that, in the end, the EU is perfectly willing to betray the very principles—tax neutrality and destination-based taxation—that purportedly command the awkward and inefficient tax regime that it has chosen to inflict on non-EU firms.

The U.S. Debate: "Simplification"?

The question of taxing remote services, which has preoccupied the OECD and the EU, has played no role in the United States, for the simple reason that intangible goods and services are generally not subject to sales or other consumption taxes in the United States.[21] The vast majority of states (as well as over 7,500 local jurisdictions), however, tax the sale of tangible goods; unlike actual countries, U.S. jurisdictions cannot intercept and tax those goods at their borders. Thus, the fear that e-commerce might evade local taxation by substituting "remote" Internet purchases for local transactions—a very minor concern in the international arena—has dominated the e-commerce debate in the United States. In all other structural respects, however, the American debate has run parallel to the international debate—and, in drearily predictable ways, to earlier U.S. debates over the taxation of interstate commerce in general and catalogue sales in particular.[22]

In the 1930s, the Supreme Court permitted states (and local jurisdictions) to levy a "use tax" on out-of-state goods. While such taxes patently discriminate against out-of-state producers and sellers, the Court justified them as "offsets" for equivalent sales taxes imposed on domestic sellers. Ever since, the problem has been how and from whom state and local jurisdictions may collect use taxes. Consumers, as noted, are unlikely to report their use tax obligations (except for purchases that are subject to independent registration requirements, such as boats and automobiles). Here, as in the international context, the seller emerges as the only plausible collection agent.

In the 1992 *Quill* decision, a case arising over the taxability of interstate catalogue sales, the Supreme Court ruled that states may impose use tax collection obligations only if the seller has a "nexus" (such as a physical presence) in the taxing jurisdiction.[23] State tax authorities and courts have interpreted this requirement in widely varying ways, some of which are very expansive interpretations.[24] It has remained clear, however, that the routine use of the postal service or local roads for service delivery does not constitute a sufficient "nexus" for purposes of taxation. The accessibility of a webserver for customers in a given state does not satisfy that requirement, either. Thus, the *Quill* regime creates a *de facto* taxation difference between local sales and "remote" sales—that is, sales by companies without a nexus to the taxing jurisdiction. A book sale through the local store—and usually even through Barnes&Noble.com—will be taxable at the local sales tax rate and be collected from the seller. The equivalent sale from Amazon.com (outside the company's home state) will be subject to the local *use* tax. But since that tax can be collected neither from the buyer nor from the company—which has no nexus to the taxing jurisdiction—the sale will in effect be "tax free."

State and local governments have implored Congress to lift the *Quill* restriction on taxing remote sales. That proposal enjoys the support of "bricks and mortar" firms and industries, which suffer a competitive disadvantage under the extant tax regime. Congress has so far resisted those entreaties. In the (misleadingly named) Internet Tax Freedom Act of 1998, Congress enacted a three-year moratorium on "special and discriminatory" taxes on Internet commerce, while leaving the *Quill* regime intact.[25] That arrangement was extended in 2001 for another two years.

Unable to have their way in Congress, states and intergovernmental organizations—the Multistate Tax Commission, the Federation of Tax Administrators, and the National Council of State Legislatures—initiated the so-called Streamlined Sales Tax Project (SSTP). The SSTP rests on the same formula as the OECD's Ottawa principles: tax all sales (including remote sales) at the place of consumption, enhance intergovernmental cooperation and policy coordination, and facilitate tax administration and reduce compliance costs. The SSTP hopes to achieve the latter objectives through a combination of centralization, harmonization, and technological innovation. Sellers, who currently have to calculate, charge, and remit use taxes in every jurisdiction where they have a "nexus" and make a sale, would report sales and the customer's location to a single entity. States would "simplify" the sales and use tax regime by harmonizing the tax base (though not necessarily the tax rates) both internally, among local jurisdictions, and across states. Sophisticated computer software, it is hoped, will permit a prompt, accurate, and inexpensive calculation of tax obligations.

In November 2002, over thirty states and the District of Columbia presented the so-called Streamlined Sales and Use Tax Agreement (SSUTA), a proposed interstate agreement that contains, in addition to its operative provisions, a seventy-page compendium of common definitions for tangible goods.[26] The SSUTA will take effect when at least ten states, representing at least 20 percent of the population, come into full compliance with the agreement and successfully apply for SSTP membership. At this writing, twenty states have adopted the SSUTA through legislation, and the SSTP states plan to meet in November 2003 to discuss the next steps toward formalization of the agreement.[27] For the time being, the SSUTA is voluntary for both states and participating industries. (States may not unilaterally violate the *Quill* restrictions on taxation of remote interstate sales, nor may they do so by mutual agreement.) After ratification by the requisite number of states, however, the states plan to request federal legislation authorizing mandatory sales and use tax collection on all sales among participating states.

The SSTP states may have shown sufficient commitment to "simplification"—and may have attracted sufficient industry support for their project—to cram such an override of the *Quill* regime through Congress, over the objections of e-commerce and catalogue sellers and their (low-tax) home states. Even in that event, however, the SSTP will continue to face intractable obstacles on all fronts—technology, simplification, and harmonization. Participating industries may well find that the expected bargain never materializes.

The SSTP has sponsored experiments with centralized data collection systems to facilitate an accurate, low-cost calculation of sales tax obligations. The first such test run, involving four states, three technology vendors, and one online seller, provided little reason to believe that such projects are technically feasible: Only one vendor managed to create a working system, and even that "successful" model provides no clues concerning the viability of a vastly larger system involving thousands of firms and millions of customers.[28] More recently, several of the largest retailers in the country, including Wal-Mart, Target, and Toys "R" Us, have volunteered to participate in the SSUTA and to collect taxes on their online sales.[29] These behemoths possess the resources to integrate their internal accounting systems with the SSUTA system. (In any event, they already have to report and remit sales taxes in multiple states.) For the vast majority of online retailers, though, existing technology cannot cope with the maze of definitions, exemptions, and reporting and remittance requirements.[30]

In the end, then, operability and general industry acceptance of a centralized collection system depend on comprehensive sales tax simplification and harmonization. Those objectives have proven elusive for decades, and not for lack of trying.[31] The SSTP will suffer the same fate, notwithstanding its modest progress to date.

Simplification presupposes universal state participation—which is not going to happen. Some states have no sales tax and therefore have no incentive to join the SSUTA. Other states (such as Colorado) aspire to becoming "high-tech havens" and will for that (or some comparable) reason refuse to join. Sales-tax states may join the SSUTA—provided that they may still protect their export industries and locale jurisdictions. Texas, for example, has joined the agreement with the proviso that the SSUTA sourcing rules shall apply everywhere in Texas except in Round Rock, home to Dell Computers. There, origin-based taxation shall prevail.[32]

From a tax efficiency standpoint (and from the perspective of affected industries), what really needs simplification is not the tax rate but the tax base.[33] Coupled with a single-rate regime, however, a common-base regime would effectively wipe out the tax autonomy of local jurisdictions.[34] The SSTP thus confronts a dilemma. Either it preserves local (and state) tax autonomy or it must make binding decisions for member states, on an ongoing basis. If it does the former, harmonization and simplification will prove elusive. (Even if the tax base could be harmonized and simplified once, political pressures at the local level would soon produce new divergences.) If it chooses the latter, few states will wish to join.

This dilemma bedevils all interstate tax cartels, and it has no technocratic solution.[35] Political pressures and intense lobbying efforts will probably induce additional states to adopt the sales tax agreement. In the end, however, the SSUTA can hope to attract a majority of states (much less all states) only by compromising its ostensible aspirations to simplification and harmonization.

"Principles"?

The OECD and the EU, as noted, profess allegiance to established tax principles: taxation at the place of consumption, neutrality, simplicity and fairness, and ease of administration. The SSTP and its supporters have pledged allegiance to the same principles. Those proclamations are typically followed by an observation that the principles may—and, in taxation of Internet commerce, often do—conflict.[36] Consequently, the principles must be harmonized and reconciled as much as possible. This thinking, though, is one part confusion and nine parts snake oil. The perceived conflicts derive from the commitment to destination-based taxation; they would dissolve in a world of origin-based taxation. Among all the principles, moreover, only the destination principle conflicts with every other principle.

Consider the perceived conflict between neutrality and simplicity. All admit that the taxation of remote B2C services and, in the United States, of remote sales of goods, poses unique and daunting difficulties. Sellers must calculate tax collection obligations for thousands of jurisdictions, and may have no practical way of ascertaining each customer's tax jurisdiction. Similarly, tax authorities will have a hard time proving and enforcing tax collection obligations. Exempting e-commerce from such obligations would keep the system relatively simple, but that would violate neutrality—since comparable conventional sales *are* subject to taxation. Neutrality vis-à-vis different industries and sales channels, on the other hand, will compromise simplicity and ease of administration. Contrast this conflict with an origin-based regime: All sales, through whatever channel, are taxed by only one jurisdiction, on the same base and at the same rate—that of the seller's home state or country.

Destination-based taxes cannot be simple *or* neutral. The simplicity point is clear: Since a destination-based regime involves tax obligations in multiple jurisdictions, it will always be more complicated than an origin-based regime. The marginally more complicated neutrality point emerges from practical considerations.

Tax neutrality, the SSTP states insist, commands an extension of destination-based taxation to remote sales. Otherwise, e-commerce and catalogue retailers will possess an unfair advantage over local sellers. The tax regime, however, will not be neutral—regardless of its scope—unless it covers goods *and services*. The SSTP states and their allies have understandably sidestepped that problem: in their uphill struggle to extend sales tax obligations, they do not need the added weight of a proposal that would draw fierce opposition from heretofore uncovered industries. That said, a selective commitment to neutrality seems politically convenient, rather than principled.

Professor Charles E. McLure of the Hoover Institution, the most relentless advocate of neutral and destination-based taxation, has recognized this point and argued for the introduction of a retail sales tax covering all goods and services, from all states and through all channels (while exempting all business purchases).[37] In view of the monumental political obstacles, Professor Walter Hellerstein, the nation's leading authority on state taxation and a defender of destination-based taxation, has described McLure's proposal as belonging to the "assume a can opener" school of economics, a characterization to which McLure has objected only mildly.[38] Even McLure, however, must ultimately surrender the purity of his theoretical commitments. Insistent on neutrality, he proposes an extension of tax collection obligations to remote sellers—and then acknowledges the need for a *de minimis* exemption "to eliminate the burden of collecting use tax on small amounts of remote sales."[39] That rule may preserve neutrality between electronic and non-electronic commerce—but only at the price of violating tax neutrality in other respects. If the *de minimis* exemption is based on each firm's total sales volume, it will favor small firms over large ones. If the exemption is based on a firm's sales volume in a given state (as McLure advocates), it will favor large states over small ones.[40] (Even small firms may exceed the threshold in New York State, whereas even Land's End or Amazon.com may remain below it in Wyoming.) Neither of these implicit advantages is more rational than an implicit preference for one sales channel over another.

Similarly, McLure admits (as he must) that the "troubling problem" of cross-border shopping introduces an unavoidable element of origin-based taxation.[41] New York consumers will board Delaware-bound buses and avail themselves of that state's zero sales tax in utter disregard of Professor McLure's elegant scheme. Their conduct presents a serious problem for all neutrality-minded tax economists: the option of cross-border shopping is a function of income and location. (It is more available to rich people than to the poor; more available to New Yorkers than to residents of Salt Lake City.) Origin-based taxation over remote sales—when the good rather than the buyer crosses the border—would extend and democratize that option. Resistance to that policy choice must be based on rationales outside the theory of neutral and efficient taxation.

Real-world experience provides further evidence that destination-based taxation is ultimately unsustainable. In the United States, local sales taxes are based on the point of sale, not the customer's residence or the place of consumption—a fact that the SSTP and its cheerleaders conveniently ignore.[42] And even the EU has, as noted, betrayed its purported commitments to neutrality and destination-based taxation: inside the EU, cross-border B2C services are generally taxed at the place of origin. That policy reflects a grudging concession to reality; the EU's refusal to extend the policy to non-EU vendors suggests a discriminatory "Fortress Europe" mindset. Either way, the corruption of purportedly sacrosanct principles is palpable.

3

The Case for Origin-Based Taxation

Simplicity

If the SSTP states, the EU, and the OECD were seriously committed to their averred principles, they would long ago have abandoned destination-based taxation. That approach, as just shown, puts all other sensible taxation principles in conflict, and conflicts with all other principles. Origin-based taxation, in contrast, largely eliminates those conflicts and—except for locational neutrality, which is unsustainable in any event—conflicts with no other principle. Amazon.com's sales would be taxed in the same fashion, at the same rate, by the same entity, as would the sales of the local book store—that is, by the state of Washington. No discriminatory tax treatment would occur unless a particular state or local jurisdiction decided, for the sorts of industrial policy reasons that often induce jurisdictions to favor some industries over others, to extend tax advantages (or disadvantages) to some sales channel or other.

Local sales in a given state or country would be taxed, as they are now, at the locally applicable rate, even if the seller maintains its principal place of business in another state or country. (An origin-based system is the equivalent of a destination-based system with a very tight "nexus" requirement—that is, a permanent physical sales location.) Thus, a company with stores in all fifty states would continue to collect, report, and remit sales taxes in all states. Those obligations, however, are identical to those imposed on local establishments, and they are in any event easily manageable. The administrative headaches, compliance costs, inequities, and political problems all arise over interstate sales, and origin-based taxation would go a long way to addressing those problems. Regardless of how and where a company's products are sold, each company will be subject to reporting and remittance obligations *for interstate sales* only in its domicile jurisdiction, and nowhere else.

While the "place of origin" for purposes of interstate sales can be defined in a number of ways (for example, the seller's state of incorporation or the physical location of its webservers), the most natural choice is the seller's principal place of business. Among other advantages (briefly described below), a company's principal place of business is unambiguous and easily identifiable. It is, moreover, already defined for other tax and regulatory purposes—in the United States, by the Uniform Commercial Code; internationally, by the OECD's model treaty and related guidelines.

Like all tax schemes, origin-based sales taxation looks more elegant on paper than it will prove in actual operation. In an interconnected world, and especially in an e-commerce environment, origin-based taxation will present technical problems and hard cases. The tax treatment of Internet sales initiated at a local store is an example; the need to provide credits or exemptions for interstate business-to-business sales (to prevent a "cascading" of sales taxes) is another. State revenue flows depend on what, precisely, constitutes a "home state" and a sufficient nexus for sales tax purposes, and states are bound to disagree on that issue. Such questions merit careful examination prior to the implementation of an origin-based system.

Comparable problems, however, arise under any imaginable tax regime, including the existing system and, for that matter, a fully harmonized destination-based system. As just noted, the United States follows an origin-based sales tax system for local sales. The easiest explanation for that anomaly is the ease of administration and compliance, relative to a destination-based system. Similarly, even the most ambitious blueprints for full destination-based taxation of all consumption, such as the EU VAT Directive and the SSUTA, contain some origin-based sourcing

rules—again, due to the practical difficulties of sustaining destination-based taxation.[43] In short, origin-based taxation promises
to minimize enforcement and compliance difficulties. Even its
opponents have conceded its theoretical elegance and practical
advantages.[44]

Objections: Complementariness, Neutrality, and Competition

Defenders of destination-based taxation argue that the principle is
essential to the purpose of taxing *consumption*. An origin principle, they say, would "conceptually" transform a consumption tax
into a tax on production.[45] That argument, though, will not bear
scrutiny. Its proponents think of a destination-based consumption
tax as a "complementary" tax: citizen-consumers may impose
local costs, or benefit from public services, for which the local
government cannot tax them directly. A destination-based consumption tax supposedly serves as a rough offset. Professor
McLure has explicitly based the case for a destination-based retail
sales tax on the assumption that public services are provided principally to households and, moreover, are complementary to private consumption.

It is strange that McLure should not care to defend these
assumptions, for they are fundamental to his case—and implau-
sible. They may hold with respect to tangible, big-ticket items
such as cars or boats (although those items are often subject to
two use taxes—on their sale, and a tax or fee for their actual local
use). But the assumption of complementariness seems untenable
with respect to local consumption of books, intangible products,
or "remote" services. True, an Internet book sale depends on a
stream of public services (such as roads) that are not easily cap-
tured. But why should one assume that all those transaction-
facilitating services are being provided by the *customer's* home
state, rather than the seller's? Viewed as a complementary tax, an
origin-based sales tax is every bit as sensible as a destination tax,
and quite probably more so.[46]

Nor is it true that a shift to origin-based taxation would imply a move from taxing consumption to taxing production. First, the place of *sale* has nothing to do with *production*. The sale of a diamond ring by, for instance, a Delaware company may be taxed at the seller's point or the customer's state (say, Texas); either way, the diamond was probably produced in South Africa. Second, and more important, the collection obligation has nothing to do with the economic incidence of the tax. One way or the other, it is the *transaction* that is taxed. Whether the seller or the buyer ends up paying the tax has to do with demand elasticities, not with collection mechanisms. In addition, the consumption tax relies upon tax treatments of savings and investment that are fully possible within the context of either tax system. The question, in other words, is not what is being taxed—in principle at least, destination- and origin-based taxes cover the same set of transactions. The question is which government winds up with the proceeds—the seller's, or the buyer's.

A more serious objection to origin-based taxation arises from the principle of locational neutrality. Under a perfectly operating destination-based sales tax regime, sellers will be indifferent to the local tax rate. The tax depends on the customer's home state, and it is identical regardless of whether the sale originated in a high-tax or low-tax jurisdiction. Under an origin-based tax regime, in contrast, the local tax rate is part of the seller's cost structure. In economic parlance, it operates like a kind of factor endowment, akin to the local transportation system or the availability of qualified labor. Sellers in low-tax jurisdictions enjoy a pricing advantage over sellers in high-tax jurisdictions, thus distorting private investment and purchasing decisions.

The response has already been suggested: Any destination-based system will contain some origin-based elements and, hence, some locational distortions. Moreover, destination-based taxation generates enormous enforcement and compliance costs, which can be reduced (if at all) only through central government intervention or intensive intergovernmental cooperation. Those conditions are not attainable even in the United States, let alone globally. (As I argue below, that is all to the good.) The point is not that destination-based sales tax systems are imperfect; all systems are. But an administratively simple—though theoretically ineffi-cient—origin-based system may, for practical purposes, be supe-rior to a destination-based system that either imposes extravagant administrative costs or requires highly unattractive institutional choices (such as transfers of decision-making authority to central or intergovernmental institutions). Considerations of efficiency, administrative costs, and institutional design all come in a bun-dle. The choice cannot be merely an academic exercise; it must involve theoretical, empirical, and normative considerations.

Perhaps because of its highly theoretical nature, the loca-tional neutrality argument has played only a marginal role in the e-tax debate. The argument that *has* proven politically potent is a variation on the neutrality theme: By rendering sellers indifferent to the local tax, destination-based taxation minimizes tax compe-tition. Under an origin-based regime, in contrast, sellers in a low-tax jurisdiction enjoy a competitive advantage. States and countries will seek to attract firms by offering a low tax rate. As jurisdictions attempt to stem the flight of business firms into low-tax jurisdictions, sales taxes will spiral downward. If sellers are perfectly mobile and transaction costs (such as shipping cost) are negligible, the equilibrium tax rate—all else equal—is zero. This "race to the bottom" argument is the sum and substance of the case for destination-based taxation and the true reason why gov-ernments consistently and vociferously oppose origin-based taxa-tion. But the argument is unpersuasive.

First of all, all else is not in fact equal. We would probably see the zero-tax equilibrium if sellers were entirely free to desig-nate their home state, or to designate their place of incorporation as their home state. The principal-place-of-business rule, in con-trast, disciplines the sellers' choices. As already suggested, sales taxes are one element in a bundle of services and obligations that are offered by each jurisdiction. A jurisdiction that provides an educated labor force, an excellent infrastructure, a favorable reg-ulatory environment, a sensible and efficient judicial system, or sufficient "quality of life" benefits may be able to exact a sales tax or its economic equivalent (for example, in the form of an income tax). An unattractive jurisdiction that drives up the cost of doing business, meanwhile, will be unable to compensate those self-inflicted disadvantages by becoming a "sales tax haven."

More fundamentally, one cannot assume that the downward pressure on tax competition necessarily translates into a race to the bottom. Under certain (heroic) assumptions, tax competition may compromise local governments' ability to finance public goods; in that event, the race is to the *bottom*. But one cannot simply assume that governments act as benevolent despots. It is equally plausible (to my mind, more plausible) to welcome tax competition as a much-needed discipline and countervailing force to local rent-seeking and interest group exploitation. Under these more realistic assumptions, tax competition reduces the "political residuum" that is available to local politicians for purposes of redistribution—without, at the same time, compromising local governments' abilities to levy taxes, akin to user fees, to finance public goods.[47]

It is true that destination-based systems also curtail some tax competition. The local tax mix, including the sales tax, will be a factor in the citizens' (though not firms') locational decisions. That argument, though, rests on questionable assumptions about citizens' and firms' mobility. The general assumption is that individuals can move with great ease, whereas firms cannot. In many cases, though, firms may be *more* responsive to changes in the local tax structure—and to advantageous changes in "foreign" jurisdictions—than are individual citizens. A 2-percent local sales tax hike may not induce an individual to move (least of all if the tax increase were to rattle through the housing market, in which case an individual homeowner could not avoid the cost even if he were to move). That same increase, though, may have a rather dramatic effect on firms' locational decisions.

To put the point somewhat differently: States compete for citizens *and firms* on any number of margins—environmental regulation, labor regulation, business and income taxes. All elements of the regulatory and tax environment operate as factors for local firms. Countless government decisions provide firms with competitive advantages or disadvantages and, at the margin, shape business decisions to locate in a given state or locality. While some forms of competition (such as targeted subsidies for professional sports teams) seem quite clearly inefficient, we generally presume that those costs are lower than those of a wholly centralized government. One would have to explain, then, why the presumption in favor of government competition should not extend to sales taxes. Or, one could argue against the presumption. Respectable arguments exist for either position. But they cannot be derived from efficient tax theory; they implicate messy empirical questions and, in the end, normative views about the proper scope of government.

Sovereignty

An endorsement of destination-based taxation implies normative and empirical assumptions about the desirability—rather, the undesirability—of tax competition. That, to be sure, is also true of the case for origin-based taxation. But the case for origin-based taxation need not rest upon (although it does of course imply) a general preference for tax competition. It can be justified on independent, institutional grounds.

The central question in the domestic and international e-tax debate is not whether states or countries may levy sales or use taxes on their own citizens—of course they may. The question is whether governments may impose the obligations to calculate, collect, and remit those taxes *on out-of-state sellers.* An origin-based tax regime permits each state or country to tax and regulate its own businesses and citizens as it sees fit. Each jurisdiction's regulatory autonomy and authority, however, would stop at the border—precisely where they ought to stop. A destination-based tax regime, in contrast, imposes tax collection, reporting, and remittance obligations on out-of-state parties. That imposition does not necessarily amount to extraterritorial *taxation.* (Whether or not that is the case depends on the economic incidence of the tax—which, as noted, depends not on the characterization of the tax or its private collection agent but on demand elasticities.) In any case, however, a destination-based regime entails an extraterritorial imposition of a coercive regime that can be enforced through civil and criminal sanctions. Such a projection of government authority into another jurisdiction is profoundly troublesome, in both the American and the international context.

Federalism. The United States Constitution rests on the principle of equal, territorial states. How does one structure the horizontal relations among those entities? One possible solution is to permit mutual discrimination, aggression, and exploitation. That answer is coherent, but it is not an option for a single *country*. The only other available principle is mutual non-discrimination and non-aggression: One state's rights must end where the next state's rights begin. Those federalist principles are enshrined in the Constitution.[48]

If it has proven difficult to make the constitutional bargain stick, it is because federalism's principles subject the states to brutal competition for their citizens' assets, talents, and business. Citizens choose their state. States, of course, would rather have it the other way around—just as every private company would love to have monopolistic access to its customers. State competition, however, is not a flaw in the system; it is the genius of American federalism.[49]

Constitutional, competitive federalism does not bar all forms of extraterritorial taxation. State taxes on hotels and accommodations, for example, are largely extraterritorial, in the sense that they are paid mostly by out-of-state visitors. Those effects, however, flow from the citizens' deliberate choice of their destination, under conditions of competition. Tourists who detest Florida's taxes, for instance, can vacation in Alabama. One can have a long and difficult debate about the precise point at which a retail business can similarly be said to have "chosen" (or, in the legal language of a bygone era, to have "purposely availed" itself of) a particular state jurisdiction (for example, by soliciting customers in that state). The constitutional line is plainly crossed, however, when one state asserts jurisdiction over a company in another state solely because the company has established a website accessible to consumers in other states.

Against this backdrop, the Supreme Court's *Quill* decision—the focal point of the e-commerce debate in the United States and the target of the SSTP—is in fact rather scandalous, although not for the reasons proffered by its critics. The decision, as noted, bars states from imposing tax collection obligations on out-of-state sellers unless the seller has a "nexus" (such as a warehouse) in the taxing jurisdiction. Tax lawyers and economists have harshly criticized *Quill* as a source of economic distortions between local retailers and "remote" (catalogue or Internet) sellers. In Professor McLure's scheme, the decision certainly looks like an artificial obstacle to neutral taxation. The true scandal, though, is constitutional: *Quill* mowed down every constitutional principle that would bar extraterritorial state taxation.[50] The only bar to such taxation, the Court maintained, is the commerce clause: The inordinate complexity of state and local tax rules, in thousands of jurisdictions, would impose an intolerable burden on interstate commerce. In that so-called "dormant" application, the commerce clause is not a constitutional bar but merely a judge-made default rule, which Congress (under its authority to regulate interstate commerce) may change as it wishes.

Such an override, as noted, is the purpose of the SSTP. The logic of that demand is quite distressing. Congress possesses the authority to create a sales tax system that approximates the objective of destination-based taxation: tax all consumption. The most direct way of doing so is to nationalize sales taxes and distribute the proceeds to the states. Such proposals surfaced early in the e-commerce debate but they have mercifully died a well-deserved death. Any form of joint state-federal taxation would eventually transform the states from autonomous actors into supplicants and administrators of federal largesse. That result is fundamentally at odds with our system of federalism. In any event, the states oppose such schemes. They wish to expand their tax authority, not to surrender it.

The next most direct path is to create a cartel among the states—something like the SSTP. If that body is to create a destination-based regime that captures all consumption and avoids distortions, it must encompass all states, which in turn means that at least some states will have to be forced into the cartel. That option is politically unacceptable and quite probably barred by the Constitution.[51] So the cartel will be capable of rationalizing sales taxation only for cross-border transactions among its members. Even in that domain, the cartel will be able to prevent free-riding and defection only if it is capable of making binding decisions, on an on-going basis, for its members.

For some purposes, we want to suppress state competition and to cartelize political decision making. But we already have a constitutional body for that purpose—Congress, which is elected and which operates in broad daylight under established procedures. We should be extremely suspicious of government by an extra-constitutional, unelected governmental organization that falls somewhere between a state and a nation.[52]

Global Governance. The power to tax is a quintessential exercise of sovereign state power. While "sovereignty" may sound like a metaphysical abstraction or an obsession among people who fantasize about black helicopters, it is neither. Rather, it is an essential principle of a liberal order.[53] Taxation is coercion, and liberal, democratic government requires that citizens know where the coercion comes from. It requires, moreover, that citizens suffer coercion only at their own government's hands—not some foreign government. A government that fails to defend its citizens against foreign impositions has surrendered its sovereignty—and, in so doing, has failed to perform its most elementary obligation.

Destination-based taxation need not compromise national sovereignty. In the case of tangible goods, a destination-based sales tax operates—like a tariff or customs duty—on items that cross a border. The taxation of intangibles and services, however, often requires extraterritorial exertions of authority—collection and reporting obligations, independent verification of record-keeping and remittance obligations, and penalties for non-compliance. Such practices reach deep into another country's governance. They presuppose consent among governments and, in a multinational context, supranational institutions with authority to make intergovernmental agreements stick.

So, when an international tax inspector shows up at an American bank, for example, to verify its sales tax obligations on services rendered in Europe—pursuant to the inspector's authority under some OECD protocol and codicil—whose fault is that? Should we blame the OECD or the U.S. administration that consented to those agreements? We should do neither. We should refuse our consent to any agreement that entails such intrusion and diffusion of authority.

Recall, moreover, that destination-based taxation requires an authority to corral potential free-riders and to prohibit defections—in the international context, something like a United Nations or OECD with teeth. That project is already on the UN's agenda, and it enjoys a measure of academic support.[54] Insistence on the destination-based taxation of Internet services pushes in the same direction. The policy demand and the institutional agenda go hand in hand.

In fact, the OECD's and the EU's inordinate preoccupation with the marginal B2C service sector raises serious questions about the relationship between means and ends. The central institutions of the EU have deliberately used policy arenas that pose seemingly intractable cross-border problems as vehicles for international integration and centralization. (Antitrust policy is a prominent example.)[55] In the same vein, the OECD's post-Ottawa agenda looks very much like an attempt to instrumentalize a grossly exaggerated economic "problem" for the sake of building international institutions and to establish a precedent to press American corporations into service as tax collectors for the European welfare states. Among all the arguments for destination-based taxation, this is the absolute worst.

4

Is Reform Possible?

Proposals for origin-based taxation confront daunting political obstacles—foremost, the opposition of revenue-hungry governments and intergovernmental organizations whose institutional interests lie in harmonization and cartelization rather than competition. Also, a transition from destination- to origin-based taxation would likely produce substantial revenue shifts. The "import" states that are always the chief champions for destination-based taxation and expansive nexus tests would stand to lose from the transition. Exporting states would stand to gain, but even they would face domestic interest group opposition. These forces explain why destination-based sales taxation is the rule, and origin-based taxation a rare exception.

Still, the cause may not be entirely hopeless. The governments' massive collective action problems, coupled with sharply divergent interests among the affected industries, leave room for sober second thoughts and principled reform proposals. Insistence on the origin principle, moreover, would bring useful dividends even if origin-based sales taxation itself remained stillborn.

In the international context, the United States should take an unambiguous position in favor of origin-based taxation of B2C services. (Most emphatically, we should never consent to anything resembling the EU's VAT Directive.) Of course, the OECD has already swatted down industry suggestions to that effect, and it will continue to reject similar advances—both because the organization is dominated by the EU and its member-states, and because it has an independent institutional interest in promoting tax harmonization. Adoption of the proposal as the United States' official position, however, would probably slow down the already-cumbersome OECD process. In the interim, it may be possible to negotiate bilateral treaties for the origin-based taxation of cross-border consumer services with countries that recognize the virtues of that approach.

The greater advantage lies in adopting the principle of origin-based treatment as a general default rule for global Internet governance. On matters such as the protection of consumer information, for example—a question that has caused considerable friction between the United States and Europe—origin-based treatment is the only alternative to regulatory balkanization or, more likely, wholesale centralization. The regulation of Internet privacy by the customer's jurisdiction compels service providers to tailor their products to each jurisdiction's specifications or, if tailoring is impossible or excessively expensive, to comply with the most restrictive jurisdiction, which will by definition reflect nobody else's preference. Since either result is intolerable to business, customers, and most countries, the destination principle will prompt centralized intervention and regulation. That, too, is unacceptable. Under an origin-based regime, in contrast, buyers and sellers will sort themselves into jurisdictions that match their privacy preferences.[56] (If European consumers are as fearful of data sharing as their governments proclaim, they will refuse to deal with American firms.) Origin-based regulation, in other words, is a kind of contractual default rule—an eminently plausible option, and the only plausible alternative to an international information economy designed by political diktat. The case for the origin principle is strong in the tax area; it is still more powerful in regulatory contexts. Principled insistence on the origin rule in every applicable context would help to advance it in each, or at least some.

America's international position would be strengthened if our domestic arrangements conformed to it. On Internet taxation (as on other questions), we can in some sense afford to suppress tax competition here at home and yet champion it in the international arena, simply by throwing our considerable weight around.

We do so, however, at the risk of international resentment and recrimination. It is much better to practice at home the competition that we preach abroad.

Constituencies in support of that agenda should advance it in future debates over federal legislation. Pending proposals to codify—and tighten—interstate "nexus" requirements might provide the most suitable vehicle. (A very stringent test, providing that nothing except an actual sales operation shall constitute a "nexus" for sales tax purposes, is the functional equivalent of origin-based taxation.) Harmonization opponents should harbor no illusions about their ability to persuade Congress or their political opponents to accept the proposal. The state and local government lobby's insistence on establishing a sales tax cartel ensures the swift rejection of proposals to institutionalize tax competition.

The most likely scenario for the future e-tax debate is a series of short-term extensions of the Internet Tax Freedom Act, including an implicit reaffirmation of the *Quill* regime. (The current enactment is set to expire this year.) That scenario is optimal for Congress, since it forces evenly matched coalitions to lobby—and to make political contributions—on a virtually permanent basis. It is preferable to a congressional endorsement or enactment of the SSTP's agenda.

Even that scenario may be unduly optimistic: one cannot rely on legislative inertia and rent optimization as a defense against tax harmonization. Transient political circumstances—the fiscal crisis of the states, continued rapid growth of e-commerce and predictions of exorbitant revenue "losses," and cosmetic progress on the states' simplification efforts—may prompt Congress to enact the SSTP model.[57] At the same time, the business coalition for tax harmonization has grown, and will continue to grow. Put simply, the bricks-and-mortar industries' demand for equal tax treatment has two possible solutions: tax both conventional and e-commerce sales, or tax neither. The "tax neither" option has no independent constituency support. The "tax both" option, in contrast, enjoys the firm support of state and local governments, which might be sufficient to obtain federal legislation.

That being so, the industry calculus is straightforward: At what point does the promised reduction of transaction costs (that is, tax simplification) justify the risk of collecting taxes from heretofore untaxed customers? Since the no-tax option seems a lost cause, even elusive promises of tax simplification and harmonization will tend to attract increased industry support.

The anti-harmonization forces' central weakness, though, is their fallback position—a status quo that they themselves cannot and will not defend. The harmonization horse will never reach the finish line—but may yet beat the anti-harmonization no-horse. To avert that outcome, SSTP opponents need a horse—a successful practical experiment.

Fortunately, experiments with origin-based taxation already exist. We follow the origin principle in interstate transactions with respect to flowers and, since 2001, mobile telephone calls.[58] It may be possible to learn from and to extend those experiments.

One reason why the origin principle has proven readily acceptable for interstate commerce in flowers and phone calls is an expected reciprocity of advantage.[59] A few jurisdictions (such as college towns) may experience a net export of flowers, thus reaping a benefit from origin taxation; a few other areas (such as those with lots of retirement communities) may experience size-able net imports. By and large, though, states are content to ignore the question ("Where Have All the Flowers Gone?") because the flows will average out.

It may be possible for at least some of the non-SSTP states (such as Colorado, Georgia, and Idaho) to launch an experiment with origin-based taxation of all tangible goods. Through mutual reciprocity agreements, the states could refrain from imposing use tax collection obligations on each other's interstate businesses. Colorado would abolish such obligations for sellers in any state that does the same for Colorado-based firms.[60] To be sure, the economic benefits for interstate sellers in each state might be fairly small as long as only a few states participate, but the costs to "Main Street" merchants and local governments would also be low. The small scale of the experiment, therefore, would facilitate its adoption. The demonstration value of an origin-based sales tax project might be attractive to politicians in states that aspire to be high-tech havens.

At a minimum, a limited experiment, conducted by willing participants, would enrich the rather sterile sales tax debate. The experiment could be tracked, and its results could be ascertained, through an accompanying econometric study. We may find that origin-based taxation presents unforeseen administrative difficulties or undesirable economic effects. But we may also find that the system works quite well, and that the sky does not cave in on state revenues and local merchants. That evidence and argument would add a new dimension to the e-tax debate.

America's ornery states are often viewed as relics and as obstacles to a new world without borders. Contrary to that reputation, the best of them might yet make a contribution to a more modern and competitive world.

Notes

1. See Robert J. Cline and Thomas S. Neubig, *Masters of Complexity and Bearers of Great Burden: The Sales Tax System and Compliance Costs for Multistate Retailers* (Ernst & Young, September 1999). This estimates compliance costs from 14 percent of taxes collected for large retailers to 87 percent for small retailers.

2. Perhaps the most sophisticated defense of a (limited) destination-based sales tax regime is Daniel Shaviro, *Federalism in Taxation: The Case for Greater Uniformity* (Washington, D.C.: AEI Press, 1993).

3. The origin principle is an efficient solution—in fact, the only efficient solution—for all contexts where contractual regimes promise to work best. In those contexts (such as the sale of goods and services), origin-based regulation will operate as a quasi-contractual default rule for cases in which the parties have failed to specify the choice of law. See Wolfgang Kerber, "Rechtseinheitlichkeit und Rechsvielfalt aus Oekonomischer Sicht," edited by S. Grundmann, *Systembildung und Systemluecken in Kerngebieten der Harmonisierung: Europaeisches Schuldvertrags- und Gesellschaftsrecht* 67 (1999). Questions involving harm to strangers—such as libel—raise more vexing jurisdictional issues, which are beyond the scope of this article.

4. See Andrew Wagner and Wade Anderson, "Origin-Based Taxation of Internet Commerce," *State Tax Notes* (July 19, 1999): 187; Terry Ryan and Eric Miethke, "The Seller-State Option: Solving the Electronic Commerce Dilemma," *State Tax Notes* (October 5, 1998): 881.

5. See Michael S. Greve, "E-Taxes: Between Cartel and Competition," AEI *Federalist Outlook* No. 8 (September 2001), http://www.aei.org/pub lications/pubID.13124/pub_detail_asp; Aaron Lukas, *Tax Bytes: A Primer on the Taxation of Electronic Commerce* (Cato Institute, December 17, 1999), 37-38; Jessica Melugin, "Internet Sales Taxation: Beyond the Moratorium," *On Point* (Competitive Enterprise Institute, March 28, 2000); and Adam D. Thierer, *E-Commerce: A Taxing Issue* (March 23, 2000), http://www.heritage.org/views/2ooo/ed032300.html. For a thoughtful proposal for international origin-based e-commerce taxation,

see Shane Ham and Robert D. Atkinson, *A Third Way Framework for Global E-Commerce* (Progressive Policy Institute, March 2001).

6. See Andrew Wagner and Wade Anderson, "Proposal of an Origin-Based Tax Solution for the Possible Taxation of Digitized Products Sold Over the Internet," *Testimony Submitted to the Advisory Commission on Electric Commerce* (November 8, 1999), http://www.ecommercecommission.org/proposal.htm; Michael S. Greve, *Testimony Submitted to the U.S. Senate Committee on Finance on Internet Sales Taxation* (August 1, 2001), http://www.senate.gov/%7Efinance/080101mgtest.pdf.

7. Organisation for Economic Co-operation and Development (OECD), Committee on Fiscal Affairs, "Electronic Commerce: Taxation Framework Conditions," Report Presented to Ministers at the OECD Ministerial Conference, *A Borderless World: Realising the Potential of Electronic Commerce* (Ottawa 1998): 4, http://www.oecd.org/pdf/m0000 15000/m00015517.pdf.

8. Ibid., 5.

9. OECD, *Taxation and Electronic Commerce: Implementing the Ottawa Taxation Framework Conditions* (2001): 26.

10. Ibid., 20.

11. Ibid., 30, 37.

12. David Hardesty, "EU Withdraws Proposal for VAT on Digital Sales," *EcommerceTax.com,* http://www.ecommercetax.com/doc/o2o4o1.htm.

13. OECD, *Taxation and Electronic Commerce,* 6.

14. Ibid., 32–33.

15. Ibid., 20–21.

16. Ibid., 36.

17. Ibid., 37.

18. The text of the directive ("Council Directive 2002/38/EC," May 7, 2002) is available at http://www.eudigitalsales.com/Directive.htm. For a concise summary and discussion, see Nigel Kempton and Taylor Wessing, "EU Tax Plan Will Affect Non-EU Suppliers," *World E-Business Law Report* (September 12, 2002).

19. "EU Taxes Hit U.S. Web Sellers," *Wall Street Journal,* July 1, 2003; "Statement by Deputy Treasury Secretary Kenneth W. Dam on European Union E-Commerce Tax Proposal," February 8, 2002, http://www. treas.gov/press/releases/po1001.htm.

20. Janet E. Moran and Jeffrey Kummer, "U.S. and International Taxation of the Internet," 712 *Practising Law Institute, Patents, Copyrights, Trademarks, And Literary Property Course Handbook Series 405,* 484 (2002).

21. Many states tax certain kinds of services, such as utilities, hotels and restaurants, and amusement centers. But there is no general sales tax on services, and state attempts to introduce such a tax (for example, by

Florida) have met with ferocious political opposition.   See Jon Nordheimer, "Florida Politicians Demoralized After Repeal of Services Tax," *New York Times*, December 12, 1987. Services of the kind that are now often provided over the Internet are usually untaxed.

22. The e-tax debate is little more than a rehash of a similarly inconclusive scholarly and legislative debate that raged over mail-order sales during the 1980s. See Paul J. Hartmann, "Collection of the Use Tax on Out-of-State Mail-Order Sales," 39 *Vanderbilt Law Review* 993 (1986).

23. *Quill v. North Dakota*, 504 U.S. 298 (1992).

24. John C. Blase and John W. Westmoreland, "Quill Has Been Plucked! MTC States Are Slowly Eroding the Substantial Nexus Standard," 73 *North Dakota Law Review* 685 (1997).

25. Internet Tax Freedom Act, P.L. 105-277, 112 Stat. 2681-719 (1998), codified at 47 U.S.C. paragraph 151. The act is mislabeled because it does not "free" Internet commerce from any tax that applies to comparable sales.

26. For a concise and instructive description of the SSUTA, see J. Michael Reese, "Does the Streamlined Agreement Signal the End of Quill In the Area of E-Commerce?" *State Tax Notes* (September 1, 2003): 639.

27. Christopher Swope, "States Approve Sales-Tax Pact," *Governing* (January 2003): 44. The current status of SSTP membership comes courtesy of the National Conference of State Legislatures.

28. Brian Krebs, "State Coalition Approves Internet Sales Tax Plan," *Washington Post*, November 12, 2002.

29. Brian Krebs and Jonathan Krim, "Big Stores to Charge Sales Taxes Online: Retailers Agree to Collect for States," *Washington Post*, February 7, 2003.

30. Jon W. Abolins, Chief Tax Counsel and Vice President, TAXWARE International, Inc., *Testimony to the House Judiciary Subcommittee on Commercial and Administrative Law* (July 18, 2001): 65, http://commdocs.house.gov/committees/judiciary/hju73964.000/hju73964_0f.htm.

31. For a description of unsuccessful simplification efforts, see Kendall L. Houghton and Walter Hellerstein, "State Taxation of Electronic Commerce: Perspectives on Proposals for Change and Their Constitutionality," 2000 *Brigham Young University Law Review* 9, 29–30.

32. Teri Rucker, "Three States Stray from Full Compliance On Sales Tax Plan," *National Journal*, August 8, 2003. Minnesota and Washington have also enacted versions of the SSUTA that do not comport with the agreement's provisions.

33. See Shaviro, *Federalism in Taxation*.

34. For an argument that even current, limited "streamlining" proposals pose a serious threat to local tax autonomy, see Janice C. Griffith,

"State and Local Revenue Enhancement and Tax Policies in a Digital Age: E-Commerce Taxation, Business Tax Incentives, and Litigation Generated Revenues," 34 *Urban Lawyer* 429, 432–38 (2002).

35. A classic example is the Multistate Tax Compact (MTC), which governs the multistate taxation of business income. For a discussion of the MTC and the logic of interstate tax cartels, see Michael S. Greve, "Compacts, Cartels, and Congressional Consent,"   68 *Missouri Law Review* 285, 333–46 (2003).

36. See Houghton and Hellerstein, "State Taxation of Electronic Commerce," 15; OECD, *Taxation and Electronic Commerce*, 11, 18.

37. A small sample of Professor Charles E. McLure's stream of articles on the subjects includes the following: "Taxation of Electronic Commerce: Economic Objectives, Technological Constraints, and Tax Laws," 52 *Tax Law Review* 269 (1997); "Achieving Neutrality Between Electronic and Nonelectronic Commerce," *State Tax Notes* (July 19, 1999): 193, 197; "Radical Reform of the State Sales and Use Tax: Achieving Simplicity, Economic Neutrality, and Fairness," 13 *Harvard Journal of Law & Technology* 567 (2000); and "Rethinking State and Local Reliance on the Retail Sales Tax: Should We Fix the Sales Tax or Discard It?" 2000 *Brigham Young University Law Review* 77 (2000). When the idea of origin-based taxation received passing consideration by a congressionally appointed study commission, Professor McLure mobilized 116 academics to urge strict adherence to destination-based taxation. See "Appeal for Fair Taxation of Internet Commerce," http://www.law.wayne.edu/mcintyre/text/appeal%20with%20names%20jan%207.pdf.

38. Charles E. McLure, Jr., "Taxation of Electronic Commerce," 277. He was responding to Walter Hellerstein, "Transaction Taxes and Electronic Commerce: Designing State Taxes That Work in an Interstate Environment," 50 *National Tax Journal* 593, 603 n. 24 (1997); ibid., McLure, "Taxation of Electronic Commerce," 411. "I plead guilty as charged, because I do not see any other way to achieve a satisfactory resolution to the problem of taxing electronic commerce." The reference is to the old joke of an engineer, a biologist, and an economist who are shipwrecked on an island with nothing but canned goods. The engineer suggests a laborious scheme to open the cans. The biologist proposes to procure sustenance from the local flora and fauna. Confronted with the practical difficulties of those schemes, the economist helpfully suggests: "Assume a can opener."

39. McLure, "Achieving Neutrality," 197.

40. McLure, "Taxation of Electronic Commerce," 400–01.

41. McLure, "Achieving Neutrality," 194.

42. Professor McLure, to his credit, has acknowledged the point: See "Taxation of Electronic Commerce," 372–73. Local sales taxation operates on the point of sale (not the destination) not only intrastate but even when the parties are from different states. If I, as a Virginia resident, buy a lacrosse stick for my son on a business trip to North Carolina, I will be charged the North Carolina sales tax. If my son purchases the next stick from the same company, which has no store in Virginia, over the Internet or by phone or mail order, he will not pay North Carolina's tax. We will instead owe the Virginia use tax—technically speaking, since neither of us has ever paid or been asked to pay that tax. Under the existing and under the proposed "simplified" system, it matters whether the stick came to me or I came to the stick. An origin-based system would harmonize the tax treatment.

43. For the EU see p. 11 above. For the SSUTA see the discussion by Reese, "Streamlined Agreement," 642.

44. For example, Houghton and Hellerstein, "State Taxation of Electronic Commerce," 54, note the "apparent elegance and simplicity" of origin-based taxation. They reject the general proposal as flawed but describe it as potentially useful for taxing the sale of digital products to consumers.

45. See Houghton and Hellerstein, "State Taxation of Electronic Commerce," 54.

46. McLure comes close to conceding the point:

> To the extent that public services are provided primarily to households and are complementary to private consumption, it is appropriate to levy a tax on consumption … as a quasi-benefit tax; *to the extent they are provided primarily to business and are complementary to production, a production-based tax (such as an origin-based VAT) would be more appropriate.* While there is no easy answer to this question, I believe that consumption-based taxes levied under the destination principle are more appropriate. If this is true, tax should be applied to all sales to consumers in a given state....

McLure, "Taxation of Electronic Commerce," 381 (emphases added).

47. The source of the term and the theory of a "political residuum" is James M. Buchanan, "Federalism and Fiscal Equity," 40 *American Economic Review* 583 (1950).

48. For a cogent exposition, see Douglas Laycock, "Equal Citizens of Equal and Territorial States: The Constitutional Foundations of Choice of Law," 92 *Columbia Law Review* 249 (1992).

49. See *Saenz v. Roe,* 526 U.S. 489, 501–11 (1999).

50. *Quill* explicitly overruled the holding of *National Bellas Hess, Inc. v. Dept. of Rev. of State of Illinois,* 386 U.S. 753 (1967), in which the Supreme Court determined that the due process clause provided a constitutional barrier, insurmountable by congressional legislation, to the imposition of tax obligations on sellers without a nexus to the taxing jurisdiction.

51. The so-called joinder clause of Article IV, Section 3 of the Constitution prohibits the joinder of two or more states without their legislatures' consent, and that of the Congress. If states may not be joined *in toto,* it stands to reason that they not be joined against their will for a single purpose.

52. I have developed the argument much more fully elsewhere. See Michael S. Greve, "Compacts, Cartels, and Congressional Consent," 68 *Missouri Law Review* 285 (2003).

53. For a terrific exposition of the notion of "sovereignty" underlying these paragraphs, see Jeremy Rabkin, *Why Sovereignty Matters* (Washington, D.C.: AEI Press, 1998).

54. The United Nations' proposal for an international tax organization can be found at http://www.un.org/esa/ffd/a55-1000.pdf. For a sharp critique, see Dan Mitchell, "United Nations Seeks Global Tax Authority," *Prosperitas* (August 2001), http://www.freedomandprosperity.org/Papers/un-report/un-report.shtml. For examples of academic support, see Jack M. Mintz, *The Role of Allocation in a Globalized Corporate Income Tax,* 36 Working Paper No. 98–134 (IMF 1998); and Vito Tanzi, *Taxation in an Integrating World* (Washington, D.C.: Brookings Institution Press, 1994), 140. For a similar suggestion in the context of e-commerce transaction taxes see also McLure, "Taxation of Electronic Commerce," 393. International tax cooperation "must include the possibility of sanctions against nations that provide a hospitable setting for those who desire to operate in a sheltered environment in order to avoid taxes on their sales and income."

55. Stephen Weatherill and Paul Beaumont, *EU Law: The Essential Guide to the Legal Workings of the European Union,* 3rd ed. (Penguin Books, 1999), 788–90.

56. See Bruce H. Kobayashi and Larry E. Ribstein, "A Recipe for Cookies: State Regulation of Consumer Marketing Information," 51 *Emory Law Journal* 1 (2002).

57. States' loss estimates have relied heavily on a 2001 study by the Center for Business and Economic Research at the University of Tennessee. The study's dire predictions include a total state and local revenue loss in 2001 of $13.3 billion, in 2006 of $45.2 billion, and in 2011 of $54.8 billion. See Donald Bruce and William F. Fox, "State and

Local Tax Revenue Losses from E-Commerce: Updated Estimates," (University of Tennessee, September 2001), http://bus.utk.edu/cber/ecomm/ecom0901.pdf, visited May 12, 2003. The results of the Tennessee study have been disputed by the Direct Marketing Association study, which concluded that the potential tax revenue lost to states is "less than 10 percent of the amount projected by the University of Tennessee study." See Peter A. Johnson, *A Current Calculation of Uncollected Sales Tax Arising from Internet Growth* (The Direct Marketing Association, March 11, 2003), http://www.the-dma.org/taxation/CurrentCalculationofUncollectedSalesTax.pdf, visited May 12, 2003. Nevertheless, Tennessee's extravagantly high revenue loss estimates have prompted many states to consider joining the SSTP. California, for example, joined as an "observer state" after the Tennessee study estimated that the state might lose up to $1.75 billion in sales tax revenues in 2001 alone. See David Hardesty, "Three More States Adopt SSUTA–California Moves Forward," *EcommerceTax.com* (March 30, 2003), http://www.ecommercetax.com/doc/033003.htm, visited May 7, 2003.

58. Terry Ryan and Eric Miethke, "The Seller State Option: Solving the Electronic Commerce Dilemma," *State Tax Notes* (October 5, 1998): 883. The Mobile Telecommunications Sourcing Act, P.L. 106–252, 114 Stat. 626, 628–29 (2000), codified at 4 U.S.C. paragraph 119(a)(2)(C), 120(b)(1). The act provided for taxation of mobile telecommunications services at the customer's address, regardless of the actual origin or destination of a call.

59. The expectation that such average reciprocity would *not* prevail is a central reason for the existing, destination-based sales and use tax system. In the 1930s, when that system came into being, "consumer" states feared that "producer" states would reap all the advantages from an origin-based system, thus leaving stranded the states that were most in need of revenues. Ryan and Miethke, "Seller State Option," 888. That concern, however, is misplaced in a modern economy where few goods are sold at their place of production.

60. The proposal may seem constitutionally problematic, since the participating states would in some sense "discriminate" among their sister-states. (They would in effect abolish their domestic use tax for goods from some states but not all states.) The Supreme Court has held that reciprocity agreements among states—unlike true state compacts of the SSTP variety, which require the transfer of state authority to a permanent interstate body—do not require congressional consent under the compact clause of Article I, Section 10 of the Constitution. The correct reason for this doctrine, although not the reason articulated by the

Court, is that reciprocity agreements eliminate obstacles to interstate commerce, whereas compacts impede or restrict it. See Michael S. Greve, "Compacts, Cartels, and Congressional Consent," 68 *Missouri Law Review* 285 (2003). See also *General Express Ways, Inc. v. Iowa Reciprocity Bd.*, 163 N.W. 2nd 413, 420 (Iowa 1968), (so holding). The question of whether selective reciprocity agreements pass constitutional muster is more difficult. The Court has struck down one such agreement under the commerce clause—see *Sporhase v. Nebraska*, 458 U.S. 941 (1982). For reasons beyond the scope of this paper, I am inclined to think that *Sporhase* is both wrong and distinguishable. In any event, it is undisputed that Congress may permit states to conclude such agreements: *Northeast Bancorp v. Bd. of Gov. of the Fed. Reserve Sys.*, 472 U.S. 159 (1985).

About the Author

Michael S. Greve is the John G. Searle Scholar and Director of the Federalism Project at the American Enterprise Institute.